CW01082684

Original Title: Stay With Me

Editors: Theodor Taimla
Autor: Jeannette Viirpuu
ISBN 978-9916-756-14-0

Stay With Me

Jeannette Viirpuu

Enduring Connection

Through the storms and through the rain,
We find a path, we rise again.
In silent whispers, tales unfold,
A bond more treasured than pure gold.

Time may falter, tears may flow,
Yet together, we will grow.
In the shadows or the sun,
One heart beating, two as one.

Distances might stretch and bend,
But our story has no end.
With every challenge, every mile,
We conquer all with steady smile.

Unending Togetherness

Beneath the stars in evening's light,
We whisper dreams into the night.
Hand in hand through thick and thin,
Together, our hearts always win.

Mountains high and valleys low,
In tandem, together we grow.
Your warmth beside me through each dawn,
In you, my strength is never gone.

Even in silence, we find song,
In our unity, we belong.
Each day, anew, our love is found,
An endless echo, a perfect sound.

Constant Companion

Under skies of blue or grey,
With you, I find my way.
Through winding paths that life might send,
You are my guide, my dearest friend.

In laughter and in darkest night,
Together, we embrace the light.
Your faith in me, a beacon strong,
In harmony, we journey on.

No matter what the world may bring,
With you, I feel like anything.
Side by side in life's great span,
Together, always hand in hand.

Infinite Bond

Beyond the realms of space and time,
Our hearts entwine, a perfect rhyme.
Boundless love in every thread,
By one unseen, we're always led.

In moments fleeting, ages past,
Our bond remains, forever vast.
A tapestry of joy and pain,
Yet still, our spirits will remain.

Through every trial and delight,
Our souls will find eternal light.
In every breath, in every song,
Together, we are infinite and strong.

Fading Never

In the depths of twilight's grip,
Whispers of the past do gleam.
Memories etched on the lip,
Of an everlasting dream.

Stars above in dark expanse,
Hold the secrets of our time.
Eternal in their quiet dance,
Chiming bells of memory's chime.

Though the day may shade to night,
And shadows stretch across our view.
Love remains, tender and bright,
A flame that time cannot subdue.

Enduring Whisper

Softly through the evening air,
A whisper calls, so faint and true.
Echoes of a love so rare,
Timeless bond between us two.

Gentle like the autumn breeze,
That stirs the leaves in silent grace.
Our hearts, forever at ease,
In this hallowed, tender place.

Silent words that bridge the years,
Transcending time's relentless sweep.
Enduring through our hopes and fears,
In whispers soft, our love we keep.

Timeless Companionship

Through the annals of our lore,
Where the sands of time do lay,
Hand in hand forevermore,
Our love shall light the way.

Mountains high and valleys low,
Paths that wind through life's terrain.
Side by side, our hearts in tow,
Together we remain.

In the silence of the night,
Or the blush of dawning light.
Timeless as the stars in flight,
Our companionship shines bright.

Perpetual Togetherness

In the dance of night and day,
Our spirits twine eternally.
Bound by love's infinite sway,
A bond as deep as the sea.

Through sunlit morns and shadowed eves,
Our hearts beat in unison.
Every breath, a note that weaves,
A perpetual song begun.

No distance, time, nor trial,
Can sever what we share.
Together we walk each mile,
In love's enduring care.

Holding Tight

In the quiet, soft as lace,
We whisper dreams, hearts interlace,
Through storms that rage, we stand the fight,
Together, dear, we're holding tight.

With every sigh, we strengthen more,
Unlocking secrets, love's deep core,
In shadows cast by moon's soft light,
We promise to keep holding tight.

Against the world, we brace as one,
A bond that's forged, never undone,
Through time's swift flight and endless night,
Our souls entwined, keep holding tight.

Love Asylum

Within these walls our secrets keep,
In whispered dreams and tears we weep,
A refuge built from tender gloom,
Our hearts find peace in love's asylum.

Through endless nights of silent cries,
We find the truth that never lies,
In shadows deep, our hearts consume,
The solace found in love's asylum.

No chains can bind this bond we feel,
In this haven, wounds can heal,
Through all despair and sweet perfume,
We live and breathe in love's asylum.

Shared Solitude

In quiet hours we find our space,
A silent world, a tender place,
With whispered thoughts and hearts subdued,
We embrace our shared solitude.

Our minds connect in stillness rare,
In silent whispers, we lay bare,
The silent bond, a quiet prelude,
Soul deep we dive in shared solitude.

Across the void, our spirits touch,
In gentle silence, we love much,
No words are needed, love renewed,
We cherish this, our shared solitude.

Unflinching Presence

Your steadfast gaze meets mine anew,
In day's soft light or midnight's hue,
In every step, your presence sure,
A love unflinching, kind and pure.

Through trials faced and battles won,
Your constant heart, the same warm sun,
In every storm we've learned to endure,
Our bond remains, unflinching, sure.

With every glance, our spirits blend,
An endless love that never bends,
Through life's unknown, of that I'm sure,
Your love remains unflinching, pure.

Endless Proximity

In whispers quiet as the dawn,
We draw close, no space to spare,
As shadows merge and then are gone,
Our hearts in tandem dare.

Breathing soft like morning dew,
Your essence lingers near,
In endless proximity, we flew,
With love so crystal clear.

Boundless moments fill the night,
Stars our silent guide,
In proximity's gentle light,
Together, we confide.

Eternal echoes of a song,
Our souls in harmony,
In this embrace, where we belong,
Love sets our spirits free.

Timeless dance beneath the sky,
Hearts forever intertwined,
Endless proximity, you and I,
A perfect love enshrined.

Beyond the Present

In the quiet of this moment's glow,
Dreams of futures start to weave,
With every whisper that we know,
We learn how to believe.

Beyond the present's fleeting touch,
Lies a realm so vast and wide,
In gentle hopes, we clutch
The paths where destinies reside.

Flowing rivers of tomorrow's dawn,
Carve the stones of yesterday,
Through them, our spirits are drawn,
To places far beyond our stay.

In endless skies of what could be,
Stars of promise softly glint,
Holding secrets that we see,
In every cosmic hint.

Together, we transcend the now,
With hearts attuned, silent plea,
Beyond the present, we vow,
To chase eternity.

Heart's Anchor

In the tempest of life's sea,
Your love becomes my shore,
A heart's anchor steadfastly,
To hold forevermore.

Amidst the waves that crash and roar,
Your touch remains so true,
In storms that shake us to our core,
Your love, a guiding clue.

Through every ebb and every flow,
Your strength a calming tide,
In the deep where doubts may grow,
Your love, my safe harbor wide.

Beneath the stars that watch and gleam,
Our vows become our light,
Anchored in a shared dream,
We sail through darkest night.

As the currents pull and sway,
In your love, I find my peace,
Heart's anchor night and day,
In you, my storms release.

Everlasting Proximity

In the silent space between,
Where words no longer need,
A love so pure and keen,
In proximity's deepest creed.

Through every fleeting hour,
In every stolen glance,
Your presence holds the power,
To mend my heart's expanse.

Timeless touch that weaves a bond,
In shadows soft and bright,
Proximity that lies beyond,
The contours of the night.

In whispers of the evening's air,
Our souls so close they blend,
Everlasting proximity there,
With love that knows no end.

In every breath, a shared caress,
A unity profound,
In never-ending closeness, bless'd,
Our hearts in silence found.

Side By Side

Through fields of green, where dreams align,
Our hearts together, paths entwine.
In whispered winds, our secrets glide,
Hand in hand, we'll walk the tide.

When shadows cast, and doubts arise,
In your embrace, my solace lies.
Through storm and sun, we stand, defied,
Forevermore, side by side.

From dusk to dawn, from start to end,
You're my compass, dearest friend.
In trials faced, and tears we cried,
Together firm, we'll never divide.

Bound by Time

In whispers of the ancient past,
Our spirits join, a bond to last.
Each fleeting second, moments chime,
Together now, bound by time.

Through ages old, and futures bright,
We merge as one, in day and night.
Eternal threads in rhythmic rhyme,
Woven tight, bound by time.

In every tick, both slow and fast,
Our union formed, in contrast.
Endless echoes, bells sublime,
Our hearts as one, bound by time.

Inseparable Souls

Upon twin paths our fates have graced,
Two stories told, one heart encased.
Through joy and pain, and fleeting goals,
Forever linked, inseparable souls.

Beyond the stars, our spirits soar,
Across the realms, we seek no more.
In love's embrace, our true roles,
United strong, inseparable souls.

Along the streams of life we float,
In every word, in every note.
Hidden depths, where love enrolls,
Our destinies, inseparable souls.

Ceaseless Affection

In endless nights and whispered days,
Your love remains, in countless ways.
Through winding roads and each direction,
I find in you, ceaseless affection.

By moonlit glow and morning light,
With you, my heart takes constant flight.
In every touch, a warm connection,
Bound by endless, ceaseless affection.

Through life's embrace, we intertwine,
In moments fleeting, love divine.
No end in sight, pure perfection,
Our love endures, ceaseless affection.

Eternal Presence

In whispers of the ancient wind,
A tale of time doth gently spin.
Through twilight's hush, the stars descend,
Eternal presence, lives within.

O'er mountains high, and valleys deep,
Where shadows dance, and secrets keep.
The sun's embrace, the moon's retreat,
Eternal presence, constant beat.

In waves that kiss the sandy shore,
In skylarks' song, forevermore.
The essence flows, without a door,
Eternal presence, to explore.

Linger Beside Me

In moonlit glow, we softly tread,
Through fields of gold, where dreams are spread.
Oh, linger by me, whispers said,
In quiet hearts, where love is bred.

Beneath the arch of twinkling skies,
In gazes deep, and tender sighs.
The world fades out, in your soft eyes,
Oh, linger by me, time complies.

With every dawn, a chance anew,
To walk as one, as morning dew.
In life's embrace, both me and you,
Oh, linger by me, shadows few.

Unyielding Heartbeat

In darkest night and brightest day,
The heart's resolve shall never sway.
Through storm and calm, it finds its way,
Unyielding heartbeat starts to play.

In valleys low, and peaks so grand,
It pulses strong at life's command.
Through every brush, and every strand,
Unyielding heartbeat takes a stand.

Come joy or pain, despair or cheer,
Its rhythm true, forever near.
With every throb, it quiets fear,
Unyielding heartbeat, crystal clear.

Timeless Embrace

In times of old, in whispers soft,
Through endless skies, and heights aloft.
Love's tender glance, a timeless craft,
In timeless embrace, we are oft.

By fires bright, in shadows deep,
Our spirits merge, where dreams sleep.
A symphony, both broad and steep,
In timeless embrace, secrets keep.

Beneath the veil of ancient lore,
Two souls as one, forevermore.
With every touch, we both explore,
In timeless embrace, hearts adore.

Steadfast Together

In the face of time's endeavor,
Through each tempest's fierce weather,
Hand in hand, we stand forever,
Steadfast hearts that none can tether.

When the sun in shadows wanes,
And the world begins to strain,
We shall rise, despite the chains,
Through the joy, amidst the pain.

Mountains high and valleys deep,
Promises we swore to keep,
Dreams to guard within our sleep,
Love in memories steep.

For the wear and tear of years,
Though life brings us to tears,
Will not dim, nor pale our cheers,
While together we face our fears.

So, let whispers of the night,
Echo softly, hold us tight,
In the dark, we find our light,
With each dawn, a new delight.

Ever Near

Through the silence, hear my call,
Echoes dancing in the hall,
In the rise and in the fall,
I am ever near, through all.

Tender whispers, soft embrace,
Gentle touch upon your face,
In the heart, a sacred place,
Within love's eternal grace.

As the world fades to dusk,
Dreams in stardust, veiled in musk,
Feel the warmth when life is brusque,
In my arms, safe from the husk.

Though the journey's far and wide,
None could break, nor could divide,
For in spirit, side by side,
Time and space, we override.

So remember, through the years,
In your laughter, in your tears,
I am near, beneath the spheres,
Close your eyes, dispel the fears.

Love's Guardian

Through the shadows, through the light,
Love's a guardian in the night,
When the heart is wrapped in fright,
It guides gently, out of sight.

Ever vigilant, it stands,
Holding tightly to our hands,
In the restless sea and sands,
Crafting dreams from life's demands.

When the world feels cold and bare,
Feel its presence, always there,
In the moments we despair,
It whispers hope, beyond compare.

Love's a beacon, shining bright,
In the darkest depths of night,
With its warmth, our souls ignite,
Chasing shadows, pure delight.

Trust in love, our steadfast friend,
On its faith, we shall depend,
From the start till journey's end,
Where our broken hearts can mend.

Always Beside

Through the days and through the nights,
In the dim and in the lights,
I am present, like the tides,
Always there, I do confide.

In the laughter, joyful cheer,
Or when sorrow brings a tear,
Feel my spirit ever near,
With you now and every year.

When the road is tough and long,
And you feel you don't belong,
Hear my whisper, gentle song,
In our bond, forever strong.

Through each trial, every test,
Know I strive to do my best,
Though unseen, I'm your guest,
In your journey, blessed quest.

So fear not what lies ahead,
By your side, where hope is fed,
With a love that never sheds,
I am here, just as you've read.

Forever Together

Hand in hand, we face the storm,
Hearts entwined, forever warm.
Through the trials, thick and thin,
Together always, we shall win.

In the darkest of the nights,
Our love's beacon, shining bright.
Side by side, we'll walk the miles,
Through the tears and all the smiles.

Ever strong, our bond will stay,
Chasing all our fears away.
With the promise, now and then,
We will find our way again.

Through the ages, love will last,
Future bright, forgetting past.
In your arms, I find my place,
Always home, in your embrace.

Heaven's blessing, love's pure light,
Guiding us through darkest night.
With each step, forever more,
Hand in hand, love will soar.

Unyielding Embrace

In the silence, hear our beat,
Love's eternal, rhythmic feat.
Unyielding, strong, our hearts will bind,
Love's pure essence, intertwined.

Through the trials, fierce and brave,
Every storm, together we stave.
Holding tight, through rise and fall,
Unbreakable, we heed the call.

Eyes that whisper, souls that meet,
In this dance, our hearts repeat.
Timeless union, strength we find,
In your love, and in your mind.

With each moment, deep and true,
Facing life, just me and you.
Fearless journey, hand in hand,
In this love, forever stand.

Never bending, undeterred,
In your arms, all fears unheard.
Unyielding force, love's sweet grace,
Found within your warm embrace.

Side by Side

Side by side, through joy and pain,
Together facing sun and rain.
In your laughter, in your cries,
Love's emotion never dies.

Step by step, through thick and thin,
Every loss and every win.
Trust unspoken, hearts aligned,
In each other, love defined.

Journey forward, paths unknown,
With your love, I am home.
Bound by dreams, by heart, by soul,
Side by side, our love shall roll.

Every moment, every while,
In your eyes, I find a smile.
With our bond, so deep, so wide,
We'll walk through life, side by side.

Hand in hand, forever stay,
Night or dawn, come what may.
Side by side, through all we face,
In your heart, my safest place.

In Your Presence

In your presence, I find peace,
In your eyes, my fears release.
Every heartbeat, every sigh,
In your love, I learn to fly.

Moments shared, so soft, so sweet,
In your touch, my soul's retreat.
Calm and stillness, pure and true,
In your presence, skies are blue.

Heart to heart, in silent beats,
Love's connection, love completes.
In your smile, my world is found,
Anchor strong, on solid ground.

Through the whispers of the night,
In your arms, all feels right.
Love's embrace, forever warm,
In your presence, safe from harm.

Timeless essence, love's pure grace,
In your heartbeat, my safe place.
Every day, your love renews,
In your presence, skies are blue.

Through Winter's Chill

Icicles hang on branches bare
As whispers dance upon the air
Snowflakes fall in silent grace
A quiet world, a cold embrace

Frosty breath neath star-lit skies
A tranquil hush where stillness lies
Footsteps crunch on pathways white
Through winter's chill, the longest night

Cocooned in warmth by fireside glow
Stories told as embers grow
Time stands still, bonds renew
In winter's arms, a world anew

Moonlight casts a gentle beam
A frosted earth, a midnight dream
In this realm of peace and calm
We find our hearts, we find our balm

Timeless Ties

In the echoes of our past
We find connections made to last
Threads of moments, woven tight
A tapestry of love and light

Whispers of a gentle breeze
Carry memories with ease
Every laugh and every tear
Create a bond, forever near

Hearts entwined, souls aligned
In the dance of life, we find
Timeless ties that bind us close
In every trial, through every dose

As the years flow like a stream
In our eyes, the same bright gleam
For connections never sever
Timeless ties endure forever

Continuum of Us

Beneath an endless sky so blue
We walk a path both old and new
Hand in hand, through time we stride
In this continuum, side by side

Moments blend in seamless flow
Years pass by, yet love will grow
Echoes of our laughter ring
In the dance of life, we bring

Every chapter, every page
In this book of life, we age
Yet our story, ever bright
In daylight's warmth and starry night

Onward through the days ahead
In every word we've ever said
Continuum of us remains
In love's eternal, endless chains

Unyielding Presence

In shadows cast by morning light
Your presence strong, our guiding sight
Through storms and calm, you remain
A steadfast heart amidst life's rain

In whispers of the night's embrace
We find your warmth, your gentle grace
A beacon bright in darkest hour
Unyielding presence, constant power

Through trials faced, you've shown the way
With tender love, both night and day
A rock, a guide, a source of cheer
In every breath, you're ever near

Unyielding presence in our lives
Inspire us as we strive
Through every dawn, each twilight's end
You are our anchor, dear old friend

By Your Light

In the stillness of the night,
You cast away my fright.
Your glow is soft and bright,
Guiding me to what's right.

When shadows loom and sway,
You turn night into day.
Your warmth keeps the dark at bay,
In your light, I long to stay.

Stars above may lose their gleam,
Their brilliance, a distant dream.
Yet you remain, a steady beam,
By your light, I am redeemed.

Love's Sentinel

Standing tall through storm and gale,
Love's sentinel will never fail.
In whispers soft, in dreams we sail,
A guardian where hearts prevail.

Through nights of doubt and days of fear,
Our faith in love remains sincere.
By your side, I'll persevere,
With love's light, we'll draw near.

No tempest wild can break our chain,
Our bond is strong, free from disdain.
In love's embrace, we shall remain,
Eternal sentinels, beyond all pain.

Never Distant

Though miles between us spread,
In dreams, our paths are tread.
In every thought, our love is fed,
Never distant, hearts instead.

When morning sunbeams kiss the dew,
Know my love is close to you.
Through every sky in azure hue,
Our bond remains forever true.

In echoes of a whispered word,
Our promises are softly heard.
United by love, not disturbed,
Never distant, always stirred.

One Breath Away

With each breath, our souls entwine,
Love's intricate, unbroken line.
In your gaze, stars brightly shine,
One breath away, you are mine.

Through time's swift and fleeting grace,
We find refuge in embrace.
In every corner, every space,
One breath away, we trace.

In moments silent, hearts unite,
Love blooms in gentle light.
Forever anchored, day and night,
One breath away, always in sight.

Shared Horizon

Upon the endless sea we gaze,
United dreams in twilight haze,
Beyond the shores, the stars align,
In your eyes, I see them shine.

Beneath the sky, our worlds unfold,
Hand in hand, each moment gold,
Whispers of the night confide,
In your heart, my love resides.

Eternal paths we tread as one,
Guided by the moon and sun,
Echoes of our laughter gleam,
In your smile, I find my dream.

No distance can our bond divide,
With you, the tides of life we ride,
In every breath, a vow we've spun,
Together, until days are done.

As morning breaks, our souls ascend,
To realms where stars and time suspend,
Endless, our horizon wide,
With you, forever by my side.

Bound by Embrace

In the quiet of the night we find,
A sanctuary, intertwined,
Your arms around me, warm and tight,
A solace in the gentle light.

Moments freeze, as whispers blend,
Promises that never end,
Each heartbeat speaks in tender grace,
In our eternal, bound embrace.

The world fades out, it's just us two,
In a realm where all is new,
Underneath the silver glow,
Our love's soft currents gently flow.

Boundless, time seems to stand,
Lost in the comfort of your hand,
In stillness, I can feel the race,
Of love that time will not erase.

Through every trial, near or far,
We remain just as we are,
In unwavering embrace,
Forever found, in this sacred space.

Plaited Hearts

Threads of fate by hand were spun,
Two hearts now beating as if one,
In patterns rich and deeply smart,
The tapestry of plaited hearts.

Twilight shadows softly blend,
The start of journeys that transcend,
In every weave and knot unpart,
We intertwine, plaited hearts.

Bound together by love's lore,
Stories etched forever more,
In sync we play each crafted part,
Joined as one, our plaited hearts.

Through storms that may assail with might,
Our bond remains, steadfast in sight,
No force can tear what love imparts,
The strength within our plaited hearts.

With every dawn and setting sun,
A new thread in our love begun,
A masterpiece that life imparts,
The beauty of our plaited hearts.

Endless time, our love will span,
Intertwined as nature's plan,
Eternal, in the artful chart,
Of two forever plaited hearts.

Cling to My Heart

In shadows where the light is low,
Your whisper softly meets the night,
A gentle breeze where calm does flow,
Embracing fear, dispelling fright.

The world may turn, the stars may fade,
Yet in my chest, your trace remains,
An endless beat of serenade,
A love unbound by earthly chains.

Hold fast to memory's fragile threads,
As moonlight twines with dawn's first light,
Though time may weave its winding paths,
Our souls entwine in boundless flight.

Stand with me in the storm's embrace,
When tempests rise with fervent might,
For what we hold within this space,
Is our beacon through the night.

Hold Me Closely

Beneath the sky, where secrets lie,
Amidst the stars that gleam with pride,
Your arms are havens where I fly,
A sanctuary deep and wide.

In moments wrought by fleeting time,
When shadows dance and shadows fall,
Your heartbeat is a soothing chime,
Resonating through it all.

The world may change, tides ebb and flow,
Yet constant is your tender care,
Through every storm, through winds that blow,
Your love remains my answered prayer.

So hold me closely, hold me near,
In this embrace, no doubt remains,
For in your arms, I have no fear,
Bound by love's enduring chains.

Beneath the Same Sky

We stand apart yet hearts aligned,
Beneath the sky that shelters dreams,
Each whispered prayer, each silent sign,
A testament to love's soft beams.

Though miles may lie between our hands,
The stars above remain our guide,
In every dusk, in distant lands,
Our spirits in the night confide.

Your voice, a melody so dear,
That travels through the void of space,
It finds me, as it draws me near,
To your heart's warm, inviting place.

And though the road may twist and bend,
Beneath the same sky, we will dwell,
For love, dear love, will comprehend,
And weave its everlasting spell.

Within Arm's Reach

Your laughter is a summer breeze,
That dances light upon my skin,
In moments close, in times like these,
Where silent words begin within.

A glance, a touch, just inches far,
Yet closer than the morning dew,
Though world's apart in who we are,
What binds us strong is ever true.

In every breath, your name resides,
A symphony of lovely tone,
With you, each path, my heart abides,
In whispered songs of love unknown.

Within arm's reach but lifetime's span,
Our hearts are locked in cadence sweet,
For in this space where love began,
Our souls in unity will meet.

Never Straying

Beneath the endless sky we roam,
Two hearts entwined, forever home.
Each step we take, in sync, we say,
Together, always, never stray.

In morning light, your smile shows,
Guiding me through life's ebb and flow.
Hand in hand, we face each day,
Unyielding bond, never stray.

As stars emerge in twilight's grace,
Your warmth, my dear, I embrace.
Through trials and paths both rough and gray,
Our love stands firm, never stray.

Autumn leaves may fall from trees,
But our love's strength won't ever freeze.
With you, my soul finds its way,
Bound by a trust, never stray.

Through seasons change, come night or day,
Our hearts as one, we find our way.
In every breath, in all we say,
Together, always, never stray.

Love's Anchor

In turbulent seas, you hold me tight,
An anchor strong in darkest night.
Through storm and wave, you are my guide,
With you in heart, I safely ride.

Your love, a beacon shining clear,
Dispels my doubts, dissolves my fear.
In endless tides, we find our cheer,
Together, always, year to year.

In quiet dawns, your voice I hear,
Whispered words bring you near.
Each trial faced, with strength and pride,
Our hearts as one, a love ride.

Through tempests fierce and gales that blow,
With you, my heart forever glows.
A steadfast soul, my port of call,
In love's embrace, I stand tall.

No matter where our paths may turn,
For your return, my heart will yearn.
In calm or storm, we conquer all,
With love's embrace, we won't fall.

Unwavering Company

In silence deep, you sit with me,
A presence calm, a harmony.
Through trials, joy, and mystery,
You're my steadfast company.

When shadows fall and fears arise,
You light my world, a sweet surprise.
Your steady hand, I clasp with glee,
In life's grand dance, you move with me.

No distant miles can tear apart,
The bond we share, so true at heart.
With whispered words, our spirits sing,
In every season, every spring.

Through laughter bright and tears we shed,
By your side, our spirits led.
You lift me up, set me free,
In you, I find my sanctuary.

As moonlight bathes the world in white,
Our hearts beat strong, in silent night.
No matter what the fate may be,
You are my unwavering company.

By Your Side

In morning's light, you greet the day,
Together, we chase dreams away.
With every step, in stride, we glide,
I'll always be right by your side.

Through meadows green and mountains high,
We face the peaks, reach for the sky.
With heartfelt love, no need to hide,
Forevermore, I'm by your side.

When rainclouds form and tempests roar,
Our love will weather any storm.
With hand in hand, our paths we guide,
In every storm, I'm by your side.

As twilight falls, and stars ignite,
We'll share our dreams into the night.
With every breath and every stride,
Together, always, by your side.

In whispered words and moments shared,
We find the strength to face the dared.
In life's grand dance, no need to hide,
For I am yours, right by your side.

Secured Affection

In the quiet of the night,
With stars peeking through,
A love that's pure and bright,
In shades of brilliant blue.

Through storms and weary paths,
We hold each other near,
Our love, a soothing bath,
Dissolving every fear.

Hand in hand we walk,
Through life's uncertain ways,
In whispered, loving talk,
We find our sunny days.

A bond both firm and sweet,
Beyond the realms of time,
With every heartbeat,
In rhythm, so sublime.

This love, our true connection,
Forever anchored, strong,
In the vault of deep affection,
Where heartbeats form a song.

Home in Your Heart

Within your heart I dwell,
A place of warmth and light,
In stories we both tell,
Our world so clear and bright.

A home where dreams are shared,
With every smile and tear,
In love, we're fully bared,
No doubts, only endear.

In corners of your heart,
I find my true respite,
In spaces where we start,
A journey to the infinite.

With every hug and kiss,
We build our sacred art,
In moments of pure bliss,
I'm home within your heart.

Together we shall stay,
Cocooned from life's alarms,
In love's enduring way,
Safe in each other's arms.

In Sync

Two hearts, one symphony,
In rhythm, we align,
Through life, a harmony,
A dance that feels divine.

In step, we glide along,
With trust as our guide,
A bond both pure and strong,
In love, we never hide.

Each beat a gentle thrum,
In sync, our pulses sigh,
With every touch and hum,
Together, we can fly.

In nights both calm and wild,
We move in perfect time,
A love that's undefiled,
A melody, sublime.

So let the music play,
In sync, we'll always be,
Through night and bright of day,
In perfect harmony.

Harmonized Hearts

In the realm where hearts unite,
We find our sweet accord,
In love, both pure and bright,
Our spirits richly poured.

With every whispered note,
Our souls begin to sing,
In verses both remote,
And close, our love will bring.

Two hearts that beat as one,
In perfect harmony,
Beneath the moon and sun,
Together, wild and free.

Through trials and through joys,
Our melodies entwine,
In moments, we're not coy,
Our love, a sacred sign.

Thus harmonized we stay,
Through every rise and fall,
In love's eternal play,
Our hearts, one perfect call.

Eternal Devotion

In the tapestry of stars, we weave
Promises that the heart believes
Through time's endless, winding lane
Our love endures, steadfast, unchained

Hand in hand, we face the sun
United as spirits, our battles won
In whispers, secrets shared anew
In quiet nights, our souls renew

Oceans rise, and mountains fall
Yet our love stands, tall and strong
In each pulse, a silent prayer
Of eternal devotion, always there

Lifetime Symphony

Every heartbeat, a note in time
Together we craft a perfect rhyme
Melodies of joy, harmonies of care
In our lifetime symphony, rare

Moments saved, in sound and light
Through days of peace, and darkest night
Each chord we play, a memory sown
In the symphony, we're never alone

Our song weaves through seasons' change
In every key, our love sustained
As one, we conduct life's grand parade
In our lifetime symphony, we remain

Forever Near

Through the whispering winds, you're near
In the gentle rain, I feel you here
Across the miles, our hearts entwine
In every breath, your presence mine

Stars align in twilight's glow
Guiding paths where shadows grow
In dreams, you softly appear
Echoes of love, forever near

No distance vast can break our tie
Under the same, boundless sky
In whispers felt, in every tear
Forever near, you'll always be

Never Let Go

In life's storm, we hold on tight
Through the day and silent night
In your eyes, a beacon's glow
Promising you'll never let go

Hand in hand, through trials we tread
With every word, love's softly said
Anchored deep, in hearts below
Bound together, never let go

Between hopes and dreams, we stride
With you always, by my side
In this dance, our spirits flow
In unison, we'll never let go

Unfading Harmony

In whispers of the morning breeze,
Nature's chorus finds its ease.
Leaves dance upon the emerald lawn,
To greet the birth of dawn.

Mountains hum with silent song,
Rivers murmur all day long.
Birds compose their joyous notes,
From tender throats.

Moonlight casts a silver hue,
As night falls, stars accrue.
In cosmic chords of universe,
Their silent verse.

Harmony in realms unseen,
Infinite and evergreen.
Through changing hues of sky and sea,
In symphony.

Echoes of a timeless rhyme,
Transcend the bounds of space and time.
Unfading, pure, and gracefully,
In harmony.

Boundless Love

Across the span of endless sky,
Our spirits intertwine and fly.
Boundless as the morning light,
In love's eternal sight.

Each gentle touch, a tender kiss,
Moments filled with perfect bliss.
In every heartbeat's subtle beat,
Our souls complete.

Through life's weaving, winding road,
Together, we share the load.
Bound by threads of purest gold,
Stories told.

No distance far, no time too long,
In love's embrace, we both belong.
In whispered words and quiet glance,
Timeless dance.

Forever in this boundless sea,
Our hearts will always, ever be.
A symphony of endless song,
Love ever strong.

Through All Seasons

Spring awakens life anew,
Petals bloom with morning dew.
In gardens of the heart's embrace,
Qhenever chase.

Summer sings with vibrant blaze,
Sunlit paths and golden days.
In every ray, dreams take their flight,
Through endless light.

Autumn whispers leaves to fall,
Colored tapestries enthrall.
In every gust, a tale divine,
of time's design.

Winter wraps in a silent shroud,
Snowflakes whisper soft and proud.
In stillness, warmth of ember's glow,
Love will sow.

Through all seasons, hand in hand,
We traverse this wondrous land.
With hearts aglow, and spirits bright,
Our love alight.

Unbroken Circles

In the dance of cosmic art,
Life begins where ends each part.
Cycles turning, time's great wheel,
Rings of fate reveal.

Oceans breathe in endless tides,
Mountains stand where earth abides.
In every loop, a sacred beat,
Nature's feat.

Stars above in constant spin,
Constellations still begin.
Unbroken in celestial dance,
In fateful trance.

Seasons change without a pause,
Life adheres to unseen laws.
In circular embrace, we find,
Eternal bind.

Through each circle, birth to end,
We are bound to transcend.
In the loop of life, we weave,
and always believe.

In Your Shadow

In your shadow, I find my place,
A world of calm, a warm embrace.
Whispers of dreams, a gentle trace,
Lost in time, together we race.

Silent echoes, secrets shared,
Unseen paths, our souls prepared.
With every step, our hearts declared,
In your shadow, no fear is spared.

Guardians of night, keepers of day,
Guiding lights, not far astray.
In your shadow, come what may,
Together bound, we find our way.

Leaves may fall, and seasons change,
Yet in your shadow, love remains.
Colors fade, rearrange,
But our bond, it still sustains.

Through the storm, and gentle rain,
In your shadow, joy and pain.
By your side, I'll remain,
Together always, our love's domain.

With You Always

With you always, through the night,
Stars above, a guiding light.
In your arms, it feels so right,
With you always, dark and bright.

Through the dawn, and setting sun,
Our journey vast, just begun.
Under skies, battles won,
With you always, we are one.

Hand in hand, across the miles,
Facing storms, sharing smiles.
In your gaze, my heart beguiles,
With you always, endless trials.

Seas may rise, and mountains high,
But together, we will fly.
In this world, you and I,
With you always, never goodbye.

Bound by love, hearts entwined,
In you, my strength I find.
With you always, undefined,
Our souls' dance, beautifully aligned.

Never Apart

In our hearts, never apart,
Bonded close, from the start.
With every beat, a work of art,
Our story, a thriving chart.

Distance grows, seasons blend,
But our connection will never end.
Through the winds, messages send,
To our love, time will bend.

Horizon stretches, far and wide,
Yet your presence, by my side.
In every tear, and joyful ride,
Our spirits, never to hide.

In our whispers, silent pleas,
Together swaying, like the trees.
Bound by fate, destinies,
Anchored souls, carried by breeze.

In your eyes, my solace stays,
Through the nights and endless days.
In our bond, no dismays,
Together always, in endless praise.

In the Same Breath

In the same breath, we speak as one,
Underneath the rising sun.
Together until our days are done,
Our unity, second to none.

Whispers carried, soft and true,
Moments shared, just us two.
In our silence, love we grew,
In the same breath, skies of blue.

Eyes that meet, a knowing glance,
In our dance, hearts entranced.
Through the rhythm, in a trance,
In the same breath, we enhance.

Words unspoken, yet understood,
In our world, nothing could
Break the bond, strong and good,
In the same breath, we stood.

Life's great waves, together faced,
In your love, I've embraced.
In the same breath, truth is placed,
Our souls, forever interlaced.

Our Endless Bond

In twilight's gentle embrace,
We find our place in time,
Connected in endless grace,
Through every whispered chime.

This journey we traverse,
With hearts forever intertwined,
A love that endures the universe,
Boundless as the wind.

Like rivers to the sea,
Our souls forever flow,
In you, I find the key,
To places only we know.

Amidst the stars at night,
Our dreams take flight so high,
Guided by love's light,
In your arms, I could fly.

As days turn into years,
Our bond remains the same,
Wiping away all fears,
Love's eternal flame.

Unbroken Chain

Through summer's golden haze,
And winter's frosty air,
Our love, like timeless days,
Lives on without a care.

In laughter's joyous ring,
And in our silent tears,
An unbroken chain we bring,
Together through the years.

Each link forged in trust,
A symbol of our might,
In storms and in the gust,
You are my guiding light.

In shadows and in sun,
Our hearts remain as one,
The battles we have won,
Prove love has just begun.

Through every twist and turn,
And paths so unforeseen,
For you, my heart will yearn,
In memories serene.

Bound by Love

In gardens where roses bloom,
Our hearts find peace and rest,
Beneath the softest moon,
We dream and feel our best.

With hands that gently touch,
And eyes that softly gleam,
Our hearts, they love so much,
Together, we can dream.

Through each and every day,
Our spirits intertwined,
Love guides us on our way,
In moments so divine.

Your voice, a soothing sound,
Whispers sweet and clear,
In love, we are bound,
Forever kept near.

By love's eternal thread,
Our souls are tightly sewn,
On paths where we are led,
Together, never alone.

Where You Are

In dawn's first golden light,
My heart begins to soar,
Seeking you in flight,
Wherever you are, I implore.

Through valleys lush and green,
And mountains tall and grand,
In all the worlds unseen,
I reach for your hand.

The oceans deep and blue,
In waves that dive and rise,
Echo my love for you,
Seen through endless skies.

In dusk's soft, fading glow,
I feel your presence near,
In places where winds blow,
Your whispers I do hear.

So in every breath I take,
No matter near or far,
For you, my heart will ache,
To always be where you are.

Love's Fortress

In the quiet of the twilight hour,
We build a fortress, brick by brick.
Strong and true, it stands with power,
A shelter from the storms so thick.

Love's fortress, unyielding, tall it grows,
With every whisper, every care.
A shield against the world that blows,
In hearts united, always there.

Through trials and tears, we'll boldly stand
Bound by trust, by words unspoken.
A realm created, hand in hand,
A bond that cannot be broken.

In every laugh, in every cry,
Our walls of love, a sacred space.
No shadows cast, no reason why,
Just endless warmth in sweet embrace.

So here within our timeless hold,
We find our peace, our bright array.
For love's fortress, brave and bold,
Will guide us safely through each day.

Together We Stand

In fields of gold, where dreams are spun,
We take each stride, hand in hand.
Underneath the setting sun,
In unity, we firmly stand.

Through tempests wild and mountains high,
With every step, our strength declared.
We face the storm, you and I,
In every trial, love is shared.

Our hearts entwined, unbreakable,
Casting shadows, none, but light.
Together, we are capable,
Facing darkness, finding bright.

As time unfolds its endless scroll,
We write our tale, side by side.
In every challenge, every goal,
With boundless love, as our guide.

So in this journey, come what may,
We'll conquer all, with hand in hand.
United strongly, day by day,
Together ever, we shall stand.

Close Knit

Threads of life, so finely spun,
Weave a tapestry, rich and grand.
Every morning with the sun,
Stitches garnered, hand in hand.

In patterns bold and colors near,
We craft a bond, true and tight.
Through each sorrow, each cheer,
In woven hopes, shining bright.

With every strand, our stories told,
Binding souls in tender grace.
A tapestry of hearts so bold,
A sanctuary, sacred place.

Each moment shared, a thread of gold,
In laughter, tears, a woven song.
Close knit, our love, both young and old,
A bond that time will never wrong.

So here we'll weave, each brand new day,
In fabric strong, with colors fit.
Together ever, come what may,
Our lives entwined, forever knit.

In Each Moment

In every fleeting breath we take,
In every dawn that graces new.
Moments linger, hearts awake,
In whispers soft, love's virtue.

With every step, we find our way,
In paths unknown, together roam.
In each moment, come what may,
We make the world our cherished home.

Through laughter's echo, tears that flow,
In every word, a promise found.
In present joy, in sorrow's glow,
In each moment, love's profound.

We gather stars in skies so vast,
In gazes locked, with love's intent.
The future bright, the shadows past,
In each moment, time well spent.

So here we stand, in life's embrace,
In every heartbeat, gently sent.
In each moment, face to face,
We find our love, our firmament.

Enclosed in Love

In the circle of your embrace,
Hearts intertwine in gentle grace,
Whispers sweet as morning dew,
Renewed with each 'I love you'.

Even stars envy our sight,
Bound together through the night,
In this realm where time stands still,
Two souls' deep connection fulfill.

Every heartbeat, every gaze,
Dances in eternal praise,
Fingers trace the map of skin,
Finding where the joys begin.

In the silence, words are few,
Yet they sing in shades of blue,
Tender moments, softly spun,
Timeless love that's just begun.

Eyes that speak in silent dream,
Flowing like a gentle stream,
In your light, my heart does glow,
Enclosed in love, we surely know.

Heart Proximity

Near or far, our hearts entwine,
Distance can't our love confine,
Across the miles, a tender thread,
Binds us where our paths are led.

In each whisper, in each thought,
Love's pure essence we have caught,
Feel the warmth across the space,
Every moment, every place.

Two beats echo, clear and strong,
In this cadence, we belong,
In your eyes, a world to see,
Drawn together, bound and free.

No landscape can shift our spheres,
Love transcends both time and fears,
In the stillness, feel my soul,
Ever near, complete and whole.

Dreams align in endless flight,
Stars aglow in shared delight,
Heart to heart, the distance braves,
Love as deep as ocean waves.

Unified Rhythm

In the dance of night and day,
Love's sweet melody will play,
Rhythms hear the hearts' soft beat,
In their unity, we meet.

Hands that hold and feet that glide,
Bound in step, forever tied,
Music sways in gentle tune,
Underneath the silver moon.

Eyes in lock, in perfect sync,
With each thought our souls do link,
Motion seamless as the tide,
In this dance, pure love resides.

Through the storms and through the calm,
Find our haven in each psalm,
In the rhythm, find our way,
Beating hearts, come what may.

As the symphony unfolds,
Feel the magic as it holds,
Ever beating, ever near,
Unified in love so clear.

Laced Together

With each stitch, our lives entwine,
Laced together, thread so fine,
Patterns rich, both old and new,
Crafting love that's ever true.

In the weave of life's embrace,
Find the beauty, find the grace,
Knit with care and bound by heart,
Never shall we drift apart.

Colors blend in perfect hue,
Every shade a promise true,
With each loop, the bond grows tight,
Lit by love's eternal light.

Woven dreams, a cherished quilt,
Layered deep with what we've built,
Every seam a testament,
To the love that time has lent.

In this tapestry, we see,
How our lives have come to be,
Laced together, hand in hand,
In this love, forever stand.

Anchored in Love

In the storm, we find our calm,
Waves may crash but we're not drawn.
Steadfast heart, a sailor's psalm,
Anchored strong from dusk till dawn.

Tides may pull, but we don't part,
Hand in hand, we walk the shore.
In your eyes, I find new start,
Anchored deep, forevermore.

Every map shows where we roam,
Charted skies and boundless sea.
Love's horizon calls us home,
Anchored safe, just you and me.

Whispered winds that guide us true,
Sail and stars in night's embrace.
We set course on waters blue,
Anchored firm in love's own grace.

Through the tempests, through the calm,
Bound by more than ties that bind.
In love's harbor, hearts are warm,
Anchored souls, intertwined.

Unwavering Bond

Roots that sink into the ground,
In the storm and in the sun.
Through the trials, we have found,
Unwavering, we are one.

Branches twist but never break,
In the whirlwind's fiercest blow.
For our love, no tidal wake,
Unwavering, we will grow.

In the darkest of the nights,
Stars above us gently speak.
Guiding love in whispered lights,
Unwavering, hearts won't weaken.

Every step, we take as two,
Through the fields of joy and pain.
Hand in hand, our path is true,
Unwavering in the rain.

In the silence, in the song,
Within every beat of time.
With you, where I belong,
Unwavering, love's pure chime.

Continuously Together

In the dance of endless days,
Steps in rhythm, hand in hand.
We move through life in a daze,
Continuously, side by side we stand.

Morning sun and twilight's hue,
Bound by threads of heart and soul.
Every moment, every view,
Continuously, we are whole.

Through the fields of time we run,
In the laughter, in the tears.
Ever two, forever one,
Continuously, through the years.

Mountains rise and rivers flow,
Paths we've walked etched in the sand.
With each breath, our hearts still glow,
Continuously, love's command.

In the silence, in the song,
Echoes of a timeless cheer.
Together we belong,
Continuously, ever near.

Heartbeat's Shadow

In the quiet, in the night,
Your heartbeat is my guide.
Shadowed paths reveal the light,
Leading close to where you hide.

Every pulse, a whispered call,
In your shadow, I am found.
In the rise, and in the fall,
Heartbeat's echo, all around.

Eyes that gleam in dawning rays,
Holding close, a silent vow.
In your heartbeat's shadow stays,
Love that time cannot endow.

Follow where the shadows lead,
Every step, in love's embrace.
Hear the rhythm, heed the need,
Heartbeat's trailing, gentle face.

In the merging of our souls,
Two shades dance as one to find.
Heartbeat's shadow makes us whole,
Love and time forever bind.

Eternal Companionship

Through the shadows and the light,
We sail on seas both calm and tight.
Hand in hand, with spirits bold,
Our story's ink in gold is told.

In laughter, tears, and whispered dreams,
With every sunrise's radiant beams,
Together through the trials we stride,
With endless love, forever tied.

No storm can shake our footsteps sure,
For in our hearts our pledge is pure.
Unyielding, steadfast, side by side,
In you my greatest joy does bide.

Seasons change as time flows by,
Yet through it all, we'll never die.
Our song of love, both strong and sweet,
In harmony, our souls shall meet.

Bound by trust, with hearts aligned,
Our journey's end will always find,
That eternal bond, our sacred ode,
Eternal companionship bestowed.

Hearts Intertwined

Beyond the realms of earthly land,
We walk together, hand in hand.
With every beat, our hearts align,
In a dance both pure and divine.

Through every joy and every pain,
In sunlit days or in the rain,
Our spirits bound by threads unseen,
In love's embrace, serene, serene.

Whispers soft in moonlit night,
Promises of love's delight.
With every breath, with every sigh,
Our hearts entwined, they soar and fly.

In gardens lush, where flowers bloom,
Our love dispels the darkest gloom.
Together facing life's design,
Our destinies forever twine.

Through every twist, through every turn,
With lessons deep, we love and learn.
In every heartstring finely spun,
Our hearts are bound, we are but one.

Together as One

In the tapestry of life we weave,
A love that others scarce believe.
With hands held tight beneath the sun,
We face the world, together as one.

With tender glances, soft and true,
We build a life for me and you.
Through whispers shared and days begun,
We forge our path, together as one.

Against the tides of time and space,
United in a warm embrace.
The battles fought, the victories won,
Are sweeter still, together as one.

In silent moments, hand in hand,
We understand, we understand.
The depths of love, the heights we've spun,
In unison, together as one.

Eternity within our grasp,
With every memory that we clasp.
In endless love, beneath the sun,
Our souls are linked, together as one.

Hand in Hand

In fields of green, where dreams reside,
We'll walk together, side by side.
With hearts that beat in perfect time,
Our lives entwined in love's sweet rhyme.

Through valleys deep, o'er mountains grand,
Our journey crafted, hand in hand.
With every step, through joy and strife,
We carve our story, shaping life.

In twilight's glow, where shadows play,
We'll dance until the break of day.
Our spirits lift, our souls expand,
Forever joined, just hand in hand.

With whispered vows amid the breeze,
Our bond's as strong as ancient trees.
Together in this world so vast,
We hold each moment, make it last.

Through every chapter, page, and strand,
We'll face the future, hand in hand.
With endless love, a perfect blend,
Our hearts united till the end.

Together Through Time

Beneath the stars, we find our way,
Hand in hand, through night and day.
Whispers of love, across the years,
Our bond remains, despite the tears.

In joy and sorrow, side by side,
Our hearts as one, a lavish tide.
Through valleys deep and mountains high,
Together we'll soar, beyond the sky.

In laughter's echo, dreams take flight,
With you, my world is ever bright.
Through winding paths and endless miles,
Together, we create new styles.

Seasons change, yet hearts entwine,
In every moment, you are mine.
Through age and time, our souls will sing,
Together, face what life may bring.

Under moonlight, hearts align,
Forever, our love's design.
In each embrace, our spirits shine,
Together, through the sands of time.

Love's Refuge

In the quiet of the night,
Your arms around me, holding tight.
A shelter from the stormy gales,
Love's refuge tells our sacred tales.

With every whisper, soft and kind,
We leave our worries far behind.
A haven where our dreams reside,
Within love's refuge, we confide.

Through tempests fierce, and skies unclear,
In your embrace, I have no fear.
Our souls in sync, a perfect blend,
In love's refuge, hearts mend.

Through darkest nights and brightest days,
Your love forever guides my ways.
A sanctuary built so true,
In love's refuge, I find you.

Everlasting, strong and pure,
Our love's refuge will endure.
With you, my heart feels safe and free,
In love's refuge, you and me.

Unspoken Promise

In the silence, words unsaid,
Our hearts converse, in light and dread.
An unspoken promise, clear and true,
A bond that time cannot undo.

With every glance, a tale unfolds,
A silent vow that love upholds.
Through distance vast, and near or far,
Our spirits meet, like guiding stars.

Without a word, our souls align,
In quiet moments, you are mine.
A promise whispered with each beat,
Unspoken, yet so deeply sweet.

Through life's chaos and calm's embrace,
Our love sustains, a timeless grace.
No need for words, our hearts reveal,
An unspoken promise, we both feel.

In every breath, a pledge anew,
Unseen by all, yet always true.
An unspoken promise, bold and bright,
Our love illuminates the night.

Where Hearts Meet

In a world so vast, our paths align,
Where hearts meet, a love divine.
In every glance, and tender touch,
We find a bond that means so much.

Upon the shores of destiny,
Our hearts converge, so naturally.
In laughter's grace, and tear's release,
Where hearts meet, there's perfect peace.

Through winding roads and bridges crossed,
In each other, we are never lost.
Together brave, both joy and strife,
Where hearts meet, we find our life.

In every dawn and twilight's hue,
Our love's unwavering, ever true.
An eternal dance, harmonious and sweet,
Our spirits soar where hearts meet.

In sacred spaces, time stands still,
With every beat, our love fulfills.
A timeless song, both pure and fleet,
Our love endures, where hearts meet.

Joined Journeys

Together we embark, our spirits high,
On winding roads beneath the endless sky.
With every step, our bond grows strong,
In this grand adventure, where we each belong.

The mountains peak, the valleys low,
Through sun and storm, we bravely go.
Hand in hand, through night and day,
In each other's strength, we find our way.

To new horizons, we are bound,
In the silence, hear love's sound.
For every mile, and every night,
We are one, in darkest light.

With each new dawn, our hopes renew,
In laughter's warmth and morning's dew.
No road too tough, no path too far,
Our journey shines, like the brightest star.

Together forever, through unknown lands,
Moving forward, with intertwined hands.
Joined in heart, and soul, and mind,
On this journey of life, so perfectly aligned.

Our Unending Path

In the quiet bloom of morning light,
We set forth anew, hearts burning bright.
Every turn and twist we face,
Marks our legacy, in time and space.

With dreams as vast as the open sea,
We embrace what comes, just you and me.
Each challenge faced and trial met,
Our journey's woeful, yet we never regret.

Through autumn leaves and winter's chill,
With you beside me, the world stands still.
In whispered words and tender smiles,
We traverse endless miles and miles.

Beneath the moon and star-swept skies,
Our bond is seen with celestial eyes.
For in the shadows, and in the gleam,
We walk together, like waking a dream.

Bound by love, and strength unspoken,
A path eternal, never broken.
Hand in hand, heart to heart,
Our unending path, a work of art.

A Single Step

A footfall gentle on the earth,
The first of many, a brand new birth.
In each bold stride, a story told,
A single step, our hearts unfold.

One step forward, then another,
Side by side, with one another.
Towards horizons yet unseen,
In fields of gold and forests green.

With courage firm, we take the leap,
To dreams unknown, and promises we keep.
Through nights so dark, and mornings bright,
Our voyage begins in pure delight.

Step by step, our journey flows,
In whispered winds and river's glows.
In every heartbeat, every breath,
Life awakens, love unsheathed.

So we shall walk, in faith and might,
Through every shadow, into light.
A single step, our story's spark,
Into the future, we embark.

Undying Affinity

In the stillness of the twilight hour,
We find our love, a blossomed flower.
With roots deep, and branches high,
Our bond eternal, touching sky.

Through seasons turning, time's embrace,
In each other, find our place.
With every tear and joyful cry,
A love so true, shall never die.

In whispered secrets, and spoken dreams,
As constant as the flowing streams.
Our hearts entwined in endless dance,
A timeless, boundless, sweet romance.

With every breath, and every sigh,
Our souls unite, as ages fly.
In life's great symphony, we find our tune,
An undying affinity, as the stars and moon.

So here we stand, forever more,
On love's vast and endless shore.
With hands held tight, through night and day,
In undying affinity, we stay.

Undying Assurance

In shadows cast by fleeting light,
Across the realms of endless night,
I feel your presence, strong and bright,
A beacon guiding, ever right.

Through storms of doubt and waves of fear,
Your voice is whispering so near,
A pledge to hold me close, sincere,
A promise timeless, pure, and clear.

No mountain high, no valley low,
Can sway the bond we deeply know,
For in your embrace, my heart will grow,
With love's eternal gentle flow.

In silent moments, when I dream,
Your essence lingers, like a beam,
Of moonlit grace, in twilight's gleam,
A sacred vow, our souls redeem.

So carry forth, through life's grand course,
Our spirits fused by unseen force,
Undying assurance, our true source,
Together bound, without remorse.

Forever Beside

Through fields of gold and skies of blue,
Together, hand in hand, we flew,
A journey meant for just us two,
With every step, our love we knew.

Beside you, mountains touched the sky,
Beside you, rivers whispered by,
With you, no dream was ever shy,
With every heartbeat, love would fly.

In timeless dances, hearts aligned,
A tender touch, a soul entwined,
Forever present, undefined,
A love that even time can't bind.

In laughter's song and tear's embrace,
In every fleeting moment's grace,
You are my light, my sacred space,
Together, love, we'll always trace.

So walk with me, through night and day,
Through every path, come what may,
Forever beside, come what may,
In love's sweet song, we find our way.

Immortal Closeness

Beneath the stars, our whispers blend,
In cosmic dance that has no end,
A love no force can apprehend,
In every breath, our spirits mend.

Through trials faced and seasons past,
Our bond's a fortress built to last,
In every moment, unsurpassed,
A love that's neither slow nor fast.

In mirrored souls, reflections find,
A truth that fate has intertwined,
An echo of the heart, designed,
To always, in each other, bind.

Through life's great tapestry, we weave,
A tale in which we both believe,
In every hug, the strength we leave,
A legacy no fate can thieve.

So close your eyes and feel the beat,
Of hearts that in forever meet,
Immortal closeness, pure and sweet,
Together, we make life complete.

Horizon of Us

On the edge of dawn, where dreams collide,
We find the place where hopes reside,
A horizon vast and open wide,
With every sunrise, love applied.

Through endless skies and oceans deep,
Together, all our secrets keep,
In whispering winds, our hearts will leap,
A promise made in worlds of sleep.

In twilight's glow and morning's rise,
We see our future in each other's eyes,
A bond unwritten, no disguise,
A journey shared, where love supplies.

Through valleys low and peaks untamed,
In every storm, our strength reclaimed,
A story written, unashamed,
Through time and space, our love proclaimed.

So let us walk, hand in hand,
Across life's ever-shifting sand,
To the horizon where we stand,
Together, in a love so grand.